STICKMEN'S GUIDE TO WATERCRAFT

Thanks to the creative team:

Senior Editor: Alice Peebles

Designer: Lauren Woods and collaborate agency

Original edition copyright 2015 by Hungry Tomato Ltd.

Hungry Tomato™
A division of Lerner Publishing Group, Inc.
241 First Avenue North
Minneapolis, MN 55401 USA

For reading levels and more information, look up this title at www.lernerbooks.com.

Main body text set in Century Gothic.

Typeface provided by Monotype Typography.

Library of Congress Cataloging-in-Publication Data

The Cataloging-in-Publication Data for *Stickmen's Guide to Watercraft* is on file at the Library of Congress.

ISBN 978-1-4677-9362-9 (lib. bdg.)
ISBN 978-1-4677-9593-7 (pbk.)
ISBN 978-1-4677-9594-4 (EB pdf)

Manufactured in the United States of America

1 – VP – 12/31/15

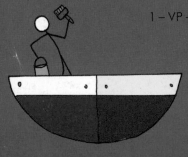

STICKMEN'S GUIDE TO WATERCRAFT

by John Farndon

Illustrated by John Paul de Quay

HUNGRY TOMATO.

At 16 years old, Australian Jessica Watson became the youngest person to sail solo, nonstop around the world.

Contents

Watercraft

Ships and other watercraft come in a vast range of shapes and sizes, from tiny kayaks for paddling on the river to vast supertankers bigger than an office block. Some are pleasure craft, taken out on the water for the sheer thrill of wind and waves. Others are the world's great workhorses, doing the vital business of ferrying everything around the globe, from computers from China to oil from Saudi Arabia. In this book, we look at how some of them work.

Shipping World

The world's oceans are bristling with boats. There are more than 100,000 registered ships overall. Half of these are large commercial ships; the rest are fishing trawlers, yachts, and other smaller craft. That's not including the countless small, unregistered boats, such as rowing boats and dinghies!

Cargo from China

China is the cargo shipping champion of the world. Seven of the world's ten busiest ports are in China. Shanghai tops them all, with only Singapore coming anywhere near its traffic. About three quarters of a billion tons of cargo are shipped through Shanghai every year, along with a staggering 35 million containers. Shanghai's deepwater container port at Yangshan is a whirl of furious activity, with a container being loaded onto a ship each second of the day and night.

Passing Ships

If you want to see ships passing, stand on the cliffs above the Strait of Dover, between England and France. More than 400 big ships glide through this narrow seaway every day, with large ferries trying to cross in between them, too. The authorities have to keep careful control to avoid collisions.

Cruising from Miami

To board an ocean cruise, the Port of Miami is the place to go. Miami is the cruise capital of the world, with more than 4 million passengers leaving for a trip on the ocean every year. There are eight passenger terminals here for oceangoing cruise ships, and all are constantly busy.

Underwater World

Somewhere under the sea right now, dozens of nuclear submarines are moving around. They are so well hidden deep down in the ocean that very few people know their whereabouts. And they can stay down for so long that in 1960, one sub, the USS *Triton*, completed the first submerged voyage around the world. *Triton* took just 60 days, 21 hours to achieve the circumnavigation.

Hover Time

Between 1968 and 2000, the SR.N4s, then the world's biggest hovercraft, whisked thousands of people across the English Channel every day, from Dover to Calais. The biggest of them could carry more than 400 passengers and 60 cars at speeds of up to 80 mph (128 km/h). The 26-mile (42-km) crossing took barely half an hour—and once took just 22 minutes.

History of Watercraft

No one knows just how long ago people discovered how to cross water in boats. But the original inhabitants of Australia arrived there by sea at least 45,000 years ago. They probably used rafts or logs dug out to make canoes. The oldest known dugout canoe, found preserved in a peat bog at Pesse in the Netherlands in 1955, is only 10,000 years old. So, who knows?

1522
Ferdinand Magellan's ship *Victoria* made the first round-the-world voyage. Magellan didn't (he died halfway).

15th century
The Portuguese developed the caravel, a ship with triangular sails that worked by sailing almost into the wind. So long voyages were no longer one-way...

3000 BCE
The ancient Egyptians built rowing barges to show off the pharaoh gliding on the River Nile, or the sun god Ra gliding through the heavens. Oarsome.

1000 CE	1150	1300	1450

About 1000 CE
The Vikings crossed the Atlantic to North America. They called it Vinland.

1580s
English sailors developed the galleon, a fast, easy-to-steer, small warship with a low front. A handful of English galleons led by Sir Francis Drake beat the giant Spanish Armada.

1793
Fulton designed the first working submarine, the *Nautilus,* while living in France. It went underwater for 17 minutes in 25 feet of water.

ROBERT FULTON 1765-1965
U.S. POSTAGE 5¢

1492
Christopher Columbus made the first voyage to America in a caravel—five centuries after the Vikings.

1791

John Fitch was an American inventor, entrepreneur, and engineer. He is most famous for operating the first steamboat service in the United States.

1838

SS *Sirius* beat SS *Great Western* by one day to become the first ship to cross the Atlantic by steampower alone. But they had to burn all the furniture and the mast when they ran out of fuel…

1787

English iron master John Wilkinson made the first all-iron boat in Coalbrookdale. Everyone said it would sink. Everyone was wrong.

1819

SS* *Savannah* was the first steamship to cross the Atlantic, though it sailed some of the way. Other ships thought it was on fire and tried to stop it.

1600   1750   1900   2000

1845

SS *Great Britain* became the first iron steamer to cross the Atlantic. Sailing ships were blown away.

1960

The *Trieste* descended to the Challenger Deep, the deepest part of the ocean, 35,814 ft (10,916 m) down. The *Trieste* was a "bathyscaphe" but clearly didn't escape a bath.

1894

The *Turbinia*, the world's first turbine-powered ship, was launched. It had quite a few fans.

1959

The SR.N1, the first practical hovercraft, was launched. Inventor Christopher Cockerell was riding on air.

*SS stands for "steam ship." It is not the sound of escaping steam or even evidence of a snake on board.

Passenger Ships

If one of the world's biggest passenger ships was stood on end, it would stretch almost to the top of New York's Empire State Building. They are like floating cities, with theaters, swimming pools, streets, restaurants, and much more. Most are built for cruising at leisure from port to port. But the *Queen Mary 2* is designed as an ocean liner, carrying people in luxury across the Atlantic.

The Royal Court Theater

The Royal Court is a full-sized theater with 832 seats for the audience, including boxes, balconies, and a grand circle. Here you can see major productions of musicals and operas while cruising the high seas.

Passenger cabins

The *Queen Mary 2* has more than 1,000 cabins, which can take 2,620 passengers. Unlike earlier ocean liners, the *Queen Mary 2*'s passenger cabins are mostly in the ship's upper decks. That means that more than 800 of the cabins have their own private balconies, far above the waves.

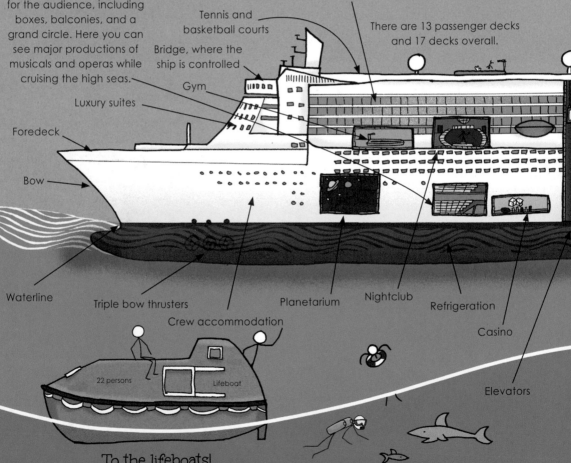

Tennis and basketball courts

Bridge, where the ship is controlled

Gym

Luxury suites

Foredeck

Bow

Waterline

Triple bow thrusters

Crew accommodation

Planetarium

Nightclub

Refrigeration

Casino

Elevators

There are 13 passenger decks and 17 decks overall.

22 persons

Lifeboat

To the lifeboats!

In case of emergency, *Queen Mary 2* has 22 Schat-Harding lifeboats hanging from davits (mini-cranes) that can be lowered in less than 30 seconds for an escape. All ships now have enough lifeboats on each side to take all the passengers and crew.

Port = the left of the ship, looking forward over the bow

Starboard = the right of the ship

Big Ship

The *Queen Mary 2* is enormous, weighing over 75,000 tons. It is 1,132 ft (345 m) long, and it would take you over ten minutes to walk from one end to the other. And, at 236 ft (72 m) high, it wouldn't fit under San Francisco's Golden Gate Bridge.

Booked

Near the front of the ship is a large wood-paneled library. It has more than 6,000 books to choose from to while away the voyage. It is the world's largest floating library.

Engine Power

The *Queen Mary 2*'s power comes from four huge diesel engines in the engine room at the bottom of the ship and two gas turbines at the top beneath the funnel. The engines don't drive the propellers directly. Instead they generate electricity to drive the electric motors outside the hull that do the actual propulsion. They also generate the power for the ship's electrical systems.

- Only the turbines are used near ports because they are less polluting.

- Out on the open ocean, the diesels fire up.

- Two of the *Queen Mary 2*'s propulsion units can swivel around to steer the ship, so there is no need for a rudder.

Covered pool

Gas turbine generators

Funnel

Restaurants

Upper deck

Afterdeck

Electric drive units

Stern

Hydraulic Steering unit

Casino

Flower stores

Grand lobby

Hull

Diesel/electric engines

Electric drive units

Propellers

Propulsion units

Sea grass

The games deck has courts for basketball and tennis, as well as golf simulators. There is even a lawn with real grass growing.

Bulbous Bow

Like many large oceangoing ships, the *Queen Mary 2* has a bulb extending in front of the bow below the waterline. This breaks up the water ahead of the bow and reduces the slowing effect of the water.

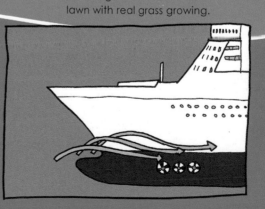

On the Bridge

Modern ships are controlled from the bridge. This is similar to the flight deck on a plane, and steering a big ship is a little like flying an airliner. The helmsman (the person who steers) is helped by an array of electronic systems. Between ports there is little navigation to do because the ship runs automatically.

Wide Vision

You need a good view to control the ship. So the bridge is high up with a clear view. You can usually identify the bridge instantly from outside by the curved panoramic window that stretches from one side of the ship to the other.

The Control Room

The heart of the bridge is the control console, with two seats and a lookout post on either side. There is also a small array of computer stations for dealing with all of the ship's other systems and the detailed business of running the ship.

Radar

While GPS *(see below and right)* tells you where you are, you also need to know where other things are—including coasts, other ships, and even storm clouds. That's where radar comes in. Radar sends out radio signals that bounce back off anything in their path. The pattern of reflections creates a map on the radar screen of everything around.

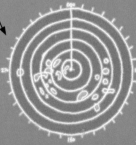

Chart table

Voyage management

The Voyage Management System is the ship's autopilot. It's a computer system that takes in data from the ship's other systems such as the engine speed, rudder, navigation satellite readings, depth readings, radar, and so on. It then controls the entire ship automatically, steering it, setting the engine speed, and so on. It also allows the ship's officers to take over manually.

Ship controls

In the middle is a console with controls for moving the ship, including the steering, the engine controls for power, and forward, reverse, and thruster controls.

Electronic guidance

Every Voyage Management System must have a navigation system called ECDIS, or Electronic Chart Display & Information System. If ECDIS views the course set by the navigator as likely to run into danger, it asks for another to be set. It posts alerts if the ship runs near hazards. And it beams out data to other craft on what the ship is doing, to avoid collisions.

Global Positioning System

Navigation means finding your position and choosing a course at sea. In the past, sailors had only compasses and the positions of the stars to help them navigate. Now they have satellite systems, such as the Global Positioning System (GPS), to tell them where they are, within inches, every second of the day.

Captain's chair

At sea, there may be just two people on the bridge: a lookout and the officer on duty. The captain and the helmsman come onto the bridge when the ship is entering or exiting a port, or in dangerous waters. The captain sits in the right-hand seat and the helmsman on the left.

Engines and Propulsion

You can move a small boat along just by pulling on oars (rowboat) or using a sail to catch the wind (sailboat). But many small boats are driven by motors (motorboats)—and nearly all big ships are driven by powerful engines. Motors and engines move the boat by turning a propeller or blasting out a jet of water.

Hybrid Power

Big ships have big diesel engines or turbines in engine rooms deep inside the hull. Most engines still turn propeller shafts to drive the propellers outside the hull directly. But some ships, including the *Queen Mary 2*, have hybrid systems. These use diesel engines as power stations to drive electricity generators. The generators are wired up to electric motors outside the hull that drive the propellers directly.

The diesel engines burn diesel fuel to create power.

Each diesel engine drives a generator to make electricity.

Screwy

A ship's propeller, or screw, works by moving water as it spins. Because the blades are twisted at an angle, they draw water in from the side and then force it out behind, pushing the boat along. Ship's propellers can run much, much slower than aircraft propellers because water is much, much denser than air.

Jet-Propelled

On Jet Skis and some other small boats, you can't see a propeller at all. Instead, the boat is driven along by a powerful whoosh of water. These "pump-jet" boats still have a propeller, but it's called an impeller—and it's hidden inside a tube in the hull. The impeller draws in water through an intake and then shoots it out in a jet to drive the boat along.

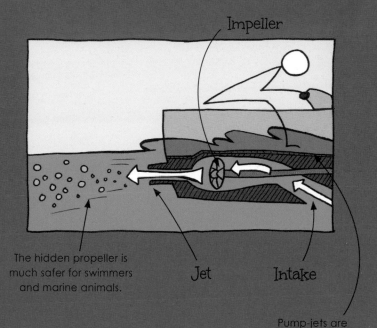

Impeller

The hidden propeller is much safer for swimmers and marine animals.

Jet

Intake

Pump-jets are much quieter than ordinary propellers.

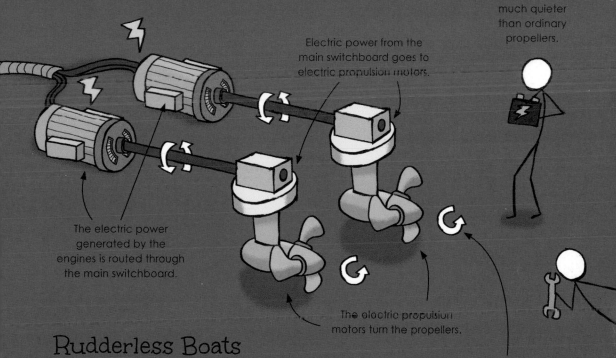

Electric power from the main switchboard goes to electric propulsion motors.

The electric power generated by the engines is routed through the main switchboard.

The electric propulsion motors turn the propellers.

The whirling of the propellers drives the ship forward as they push water out of the way.

Rudderless Boats

Some electric propulsion motors, called azimuth thrusters, can be swiveled in almost any direction. That means the ship can be propelled in almost any direction, which makes it much more maneuverable in tight situations. And there is no need for a rudder at all.

Hulls and Hydrofoils

A boat's hull is the part that sits in the water and keeps the boat afloat. It doesn't sit on top of the water but instead sinks a little way in, and as it does, it pushes water out of the way—but the water pushes back. Because the hull is hollow, it is actually quite light compared to the weight of water pushed out of the way. So the weight of all that water pushing back is enough to keep the boat floating.

Hull Shapes

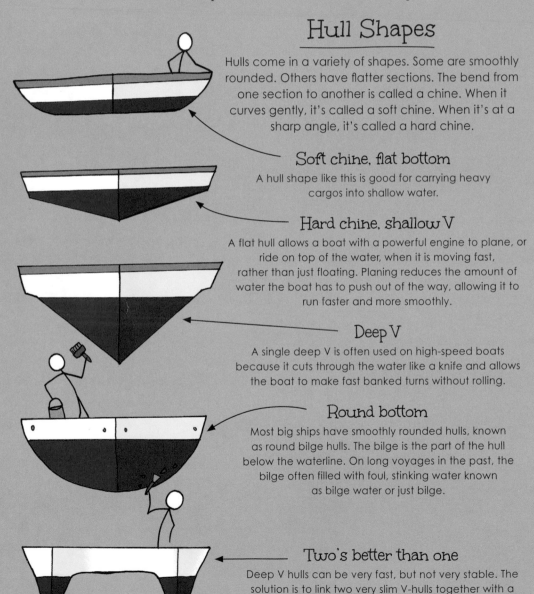

Hulls come in a variety of shapes. Some are smoothly rounded. Others have flatter sections. The bend from one section to another is called a chine. When it curves gently, it's called a soft chine. When it's at a sharp angle, it's called a hard chine.

Soft chine, flat bottom

A hull shape like this is good for carrying heavy cargos into shallow water.

Hard chine, shallow V

A flat hull allows a boat with a powerful engine to plane, or ride on top of the water, when it is moving fast, rather than just floating. Planing reduces the amount of water the boat has to push out of the way, allowing it to run faster and more smoothly.

Deep V

A single deep V is often used on high-speed boats because it cuts through the water like a knife and allows the boat to make fast banked turns without rolling.

Round bottom

Most big ships have smoothly rounded hulls, known as round bilge hulls. The bilge is the part of the hull below the waterline. On long voyages in the past, the bilge often filled with foul, stinking water known as bilge water or just bilge.

Two's better than one

Deep V hulls can be very fast, but not very stable. The solution is to link two very slim V-hulls together with a bridge to create a twin-hulled boat or catamaran.

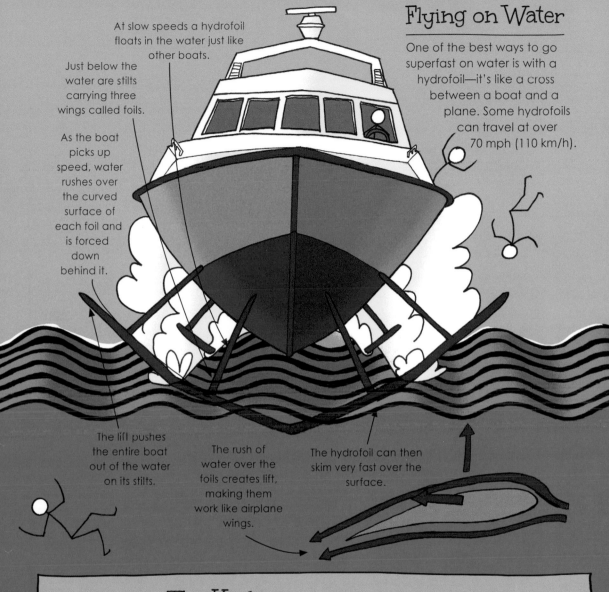

At slow speeds a hydrofoil floats in the water just like other boats.

Just below the water are stilts carrying three wings called foils.

As the boat picks up speed, water rushes over the curved surface of each foil and is forced down behind it.

Flying on Water

One of the best ways to go superfast on water is with a hydrofoil—it's like a cross between a boat and a plane. Some hydrofoils can travel at over 70 mph (110 km/h).

The lift pushes the entire boat out of the water on its stilts.

The rush of water over the foils creates lift, making them work like airplane wings.

The hydrofoil can then skim very fast over the surface.

The Keel

Every boat has a backbone, known as the keel, running from front to back at the bottom of the boat. Boatbuilding always starts with the laying down of the keel. Then ribs are attached to the keel, and planks or plates are laid over the ribs to create the hull.

On some boats, especially sailboats, the keel extends to form a fin to help keep the boat from rolling over.

In modern steel boats, the ribs extend across the hull as thick walls, known as bulkheads, which not only give the hull extra strength but also stop water from filling the entire hull if it should spring a leak.

Aircraft Carriers

The flight deck of a big aircraft carrier is a noisy, dangerous, and exciting place. When a major mission is on, there is an incredible racket from the roar of the jets. Every 25 seconds, a plane is loaded into the catapult and then shot along the deck and out over the sea—and, with luck, away...

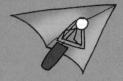

Flight deck

The top of an aircraft carrier is almost entirely flight deck—a vast, flat space for the planes to take off and land. On a big US Navy carrier, the deck is often almost as long as the Empire State Building is high (over 1,000 ft/300 m), and a football field would nearly fit across it (300 ft/90 m)!

Radar systems

An aircraft carrier doesn't just need the radar and other equipment that ordinary ships use for navigation. It must have all the systems for tracking and guiding dozens of planes in the air. It also has to monitor enemy activity. So the tops of the ship's islands (operational towers) bristle with an array of radar and communications antennae.

Bridge

Elevator

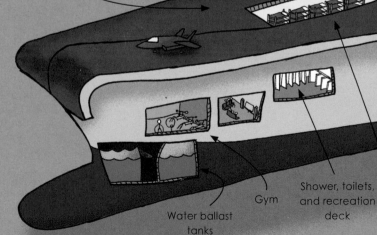

Shower, toilets, and recreation deck

Forward engine room

Gym

Water ballast tanks

Slingshot

Despite its length, the flight deck is not long enough for a normal takeoff. So planes are given a kick-start with a catapult wire attached to the nose. High-pressure steam pistons fling the plane up to 165 mph (265 km/h) in just two seconds before the wires are dropped and the plane takes off.

Racked up

Ordinary crew members don't have their own bedrooms. They have to share a compartment with about 60 other people, all sleeping in single bunks. The bunks are called racks because they're crammed together in stacks of three.

The islands

There's very little superstructure on a carrier—just the two islands. The ship is controlled from the tower at the front. This is where the captain is in charge. The rear island is the flight control for the planes. Here the air boss rules the roost.

Air traffic control

Jet blast deflector used during takeoff

Hooked

The flight deck isn't long enough for a landing, either. So planes each have a hook dangling from the tail. It's the pilot's tricky task to catch the hook on arrestor wires stretched across the deck when coming in to land. That way the plane will be brought to a halt before shooting off the other end of the deck!

Some fighter planes can take off or land vertically, without using arrestor wires.

Rudder

Officers' quarters

The officers live in slightly more spacious rooms at the rear of the ship.

Propeller

Senior ratings' dining room

Stabilizer

Aft engine rooms

Water tanks

Catering

Hospital

Aircraft carriers may be involved in combat, so most have full-sized hospitals to cope with casualties. A typical carrier has a hospital with 50 or more beds, several operating theaters, and intensive care units.

Hangar deck

There's only room for a few planes up on deck. Most planes are stored down on the hangar deck when not in use. It's two decks down and absolutely vast. On a big carrier, 60 or more planes may be lined up here, ready to be moved into one of the four giant elevators and up to the flight deck.

The Crew

It takes a lot of people to run a carrier. There are 2,500 men and women who fly and maintain the aircraft, and more than 3,000 more to keep the ship running. That means the galleys have to serve 18,000 meals a day to keep them fed!

Help, I'm Lost!

With thousands of compartments and numerous decks, it's easy to get lost on a carrier. So on some, every sailor has a phone app to show exactly where he or she is!

Cargo Ships

The world's largest container ship, the MSC *Oscar*, is ginormous. It weighs nearly 200,000 tons. Stand it on end and it would reach much higher even than London's Shard skyscraper. And it can carry 19,224 containers. It could carry enough new washing machines to give one to every single home in Los Angeles!

What are Containers?

Containers are standard-sized steel boxes for carrying cargo. They come in 20-ft (6-m) and 40-ft (12-m) versions. Because they're all the same size, they can be loaded and unloaded by the same cranes anywhere and stacked up like vast brick walls.

The ship towers taller than a 25-story apartment building.

Everything is so automated that the ship needs a crew of just 25.

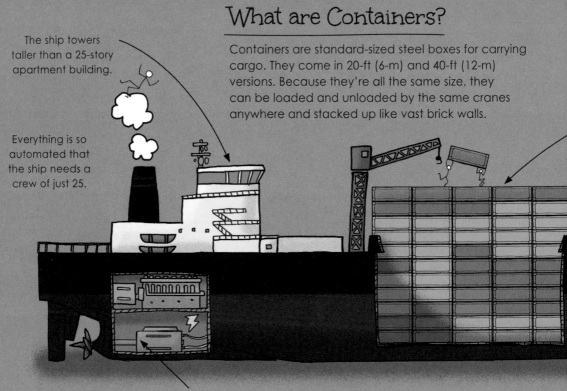

The diesel engines that power giant container ships are the largest engines ever built.

TEUs means "twenty-foot equivalent units": the number of containers a ship can carry.

1st Generation pre-1960–1970 500–800 TEUs	2nd Generation 1971–1980 1,000–2,500 TEUs	3rd Generation 1980–1988 3,000–4,000 TEUs	4th Generation 1988–2000 4,000–5,000 TEUs	5th Generation 2000–2005 5,000–8,000 TEUs	6th Generation 2006–2015 11,000–14,500 TEUs

Ship to Truck

Trucks and trains are built to take containers exactly as they are. So cranes can simply whisk the containers off a ship and onto a truck. There's no need to open them at all. Computerized numbering is vital for keeping track of them, though!

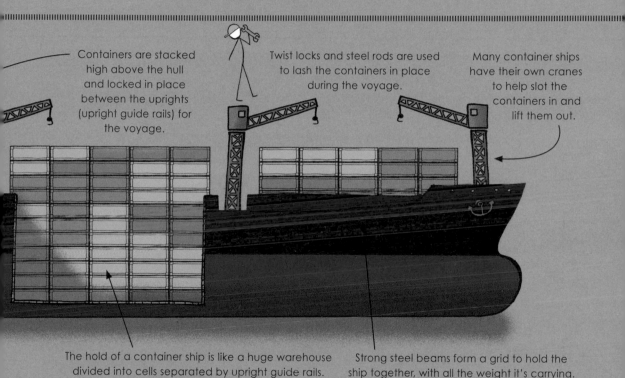

Containers are stacked high above the hull and locked in place between the uprights (upright guide rails) for the voyage.

Twist locks and steel rods are used to lash the containers in place during the voyage.

Many container ships have their own cranes to help slot the containers in and lift them out.

The hold of a container ship is like a huge warehouse divided into cells separated by upright guide rails.

Strong steel beams form a grid to hold the ship together, with all the weight it's carrying.

Container Generations

The first container ships appeared in 1956 and could carry fewer than 1,000 containers. Since then they've gotten bigger and bigger and bigger. Until 1985, shipbuilders were limited by the size of ship that could fit through the Panama Canal. Then they decided it was better to build vast and take the long route around South America. The 7th-generation ships now being built may carry up to 30,000 containers!

Bulk Carriers

"Bulk" means loose and liquid materials, such as iron ore or oil. These don't need containers; they can simply be poured into the ship's hold or tank. Oil tankers built in the 1970s, known as supertankers, were the largest ships ever built. Some were over 1,500 ft (450 m) long and weighed 350,000 tons. Each could carry 60 million gallons (272 million liters) of crude oil—enough to supply the entire UK for well over a day.

Sailboats

For many people, nothing can beat the sheer thrill of being driven along by the wind alone in a yacht or a sailing dinghy. Using the wind to push the boat in the direction you want to go requires considerable skill, but that's what makes it so fun.

Wind-Driven

Many large sailing ships in the past had square sails set across the ship at right angles. With these, the ship was simply blown along in front of the wind. But the triangular sails on yachts work differently. They are in line with the boat, not across it, and the sail functions like an aircraft's wing.

Raised pressure

As the wind blows over the sail, the sail bows out.

The flow of air over the curved sail creates a sideways force, just as an aircraft's wings create lift.

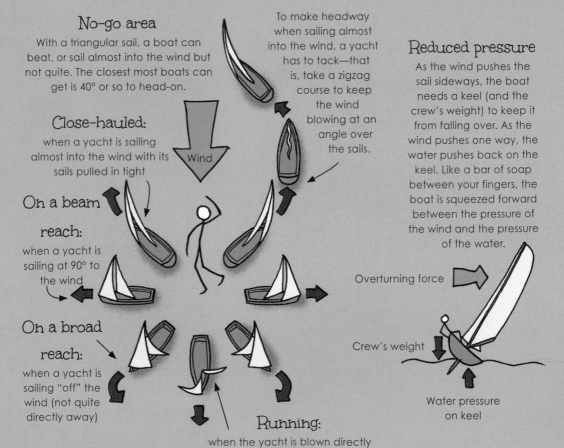

No-go area

With a triangular sail, a boat can beat, or sail almost into the wind but not quite. The closest most boats can get is 40° or so to head-on.

To make headway when sailing almost into the wind, a yacht has to tack—that is, take a zigzag course to keep the wind blowing at an angle over the sails.

Reduced pressure

As the wind pushes the sail sideways, the boat needs a keel (and the crew's weight) to keep it from falling over. As the wind pushes one way, the water pushes back on the keel. Like a bar of soap between your fingers, the boat is squeezed forward between the pressure of the wind and the pressure of the water.

Close-hauled:

when a yacht is sailing almost into the wind with its sails pulled in tight

Wind

On a beam reach:

when a yacht is sailing at 90° to the wind

Overturning force

Crew's weight

On a broad reach:

when a yacht is sailing "off" the wind (not quite directly away)

Water pressure on keel

Running:

when the yacht is blown directly before the wind

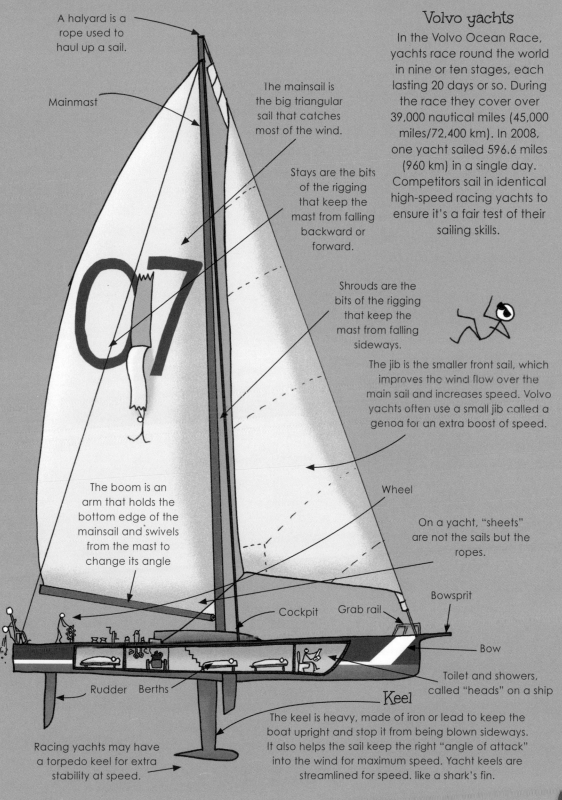

A halyard is a rope used to haul up a sail.

Mainmast

The mainsail is the big triangular sail that catches most of the wind.

Stays are the bits of the rigging that keep the mast from falling backward or forward.

Volvo yachts

In the Volvo Ocean Race, yachts race round the world in nine or ten stages, each lasting 20 days or so. During the race they cover over 39,000 nautical miles (45,000 miles/72,400 km). In 2008, one yacht sailed 596.6 miles (960 km) in a single day. Competitors sail in identical high-speed racing yachts to ensure it's a fair test of their sailing skills.

Shrouds are the bits of the rigging that keep the mast from falling sideways.

The jib is the smaller front sail, which improves the wind flow over the main sail and increases speed. Volvo yachts often use a small jib called a genoa for an extra boost of speed.

The boom is an arm that holds the bottom edge of the mainsail and swivels from the mast to change its angle

Wheel

On a yacht, "sheets" are not the sails but the ropes.

Bowsprit

Cockpit

Grab rail

Bow

Rudder   Berths

Toilet and showers, called "heads" on a ship

Keel

Racing yachts may have a torpedo keel for extra stability at speed.

The keel is heavy, made of iron or lead to keep the boat upright and stop it from being blown sideways. It also helps the sail keep the right "angle of attack" into the wind for maximum speed. Yacht keels are streamlined for speed. like a shark's fin.

23

Submarines

Modern nuclear submarines are the most secretive craft on Earth. They can dive at least 800 ft (240 m) down and travel at almost 30 mph (50 km/h). They can stay submerged continuously for three months, during which time they could travel almost twice around the world. They can go anywhere, and because they're hidden beneath the water, no one ever knows where they are...

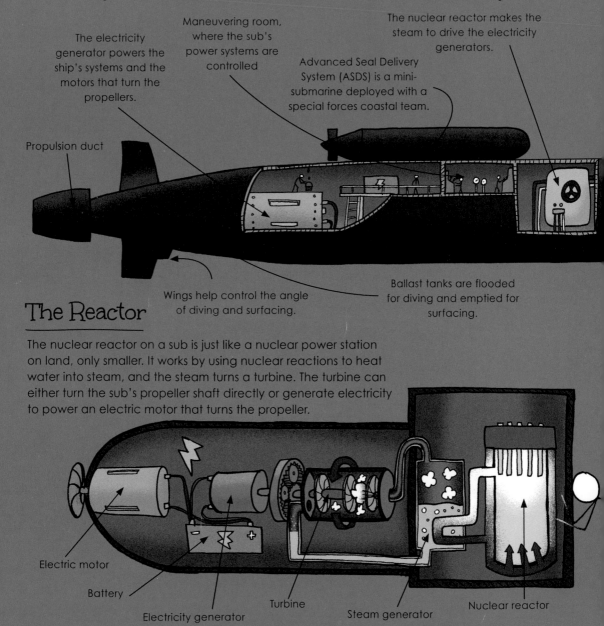

The electricity generator powers the ship's systems and the motors that turn the propellers.

Maneuvering room, where the sub's power systems are controlled

The nuclear reactor makes the steam to drive the electricity generators.

Advanced Seal Delivery System (ASDS) is a mini-submarine deployed with a special forces coastal team.

Propulsion duct

Wings help control the angle of diving and surfacing.

Ballast tanks are flooded for diving and emptied for surfacing.

The Reactor

The nuclear reactor on a sub is just like a nuclear power station on land, only smaller. It works by using nuclear reactions to heat water into steam, and the steam turns a turbine. The turbine can either turn the sub's propeller shaft directly or generate electricity to power an electric motor that turns the propeller.

Electric motor

Battery

Electricity generator

Turbine

Steam generator

Nuclear reactor

Diesel vs. Nuclear

Submarines powered by diesel engines can only stay underwater for a few days. That's because diesel engines need air to work. So once a diesel sub's submerged, it runs on battery-powered electric motors, which need recharging at the surface after a few days. Diesel fuel is also very bulky, so a diesel submarine can only carry enough fuel to last a few weeks.

Nuclear subs are very expensive to build. But nuclear reactors give power without using any air, and the fuel they need is so concentrated that a nuclear submarine could sail for years without refueling. The only reason a nuclear sub has to come up after 90 days is because the crew get hungry...

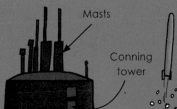

Cramped crew quarters, where the submariners sleep in bunks when not on duty

The command center, where the officers see what's going on up top on big screens fed by fiber-optic systems from the surface

Masts

Conning tower

Missile tubes for launching missiles straight up

Missile room, where missiles are stored, ready for loading into tubes

Missiles are fired from missile tubes at the front.

Retractable bow planes, together with the wings at the rear of the submarine, control the submarine's depth.

Sonar for detecting other submarines and obstacles underwater

A vent lets air out to allow the tanks to be filled with water for diving.

Trim tanks at either end are filled with water or emptied to keep the submarine level.

Wings on the side of the sub control the diving angle.

Going Down!

The key to a sub's ability to dive and surface is its double skin. In between the inner and the outer skin are large spaces that can hold water, called ballast tanks. To dive, the sub pumps water in to flood these tanks, making the sub heavy enough to sink. To surface, it simply pumps the water out again.

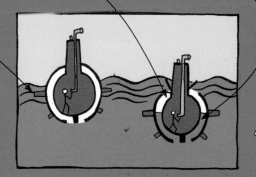

Deep Diver

Submarines can go down only about 1,000 ft (300 m). Yet the deepest part of the ocean is almost 36,000 ft (10,900 m) deep. To explore this far, you need a very special craft. Amazingly, in 1960 Jacques Piccard and Don Walsh made it to the very bottom in the bathyscaphe *Trieste*. To repeat this feat in 2012, filmmaker James Cameron used the remarkable submersible *Deepsea Challenger*.

What is a Submersible?

Submarines can operate entirely by themselves. Submersibles are small underwater craft that need a support crew on the surface to control them, or to supply power or air. The best-known submersible is the ocean research vessel *Alvin*, which has been carrying researchers into the deep for more than half a century.

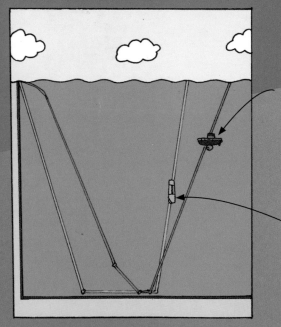

The *Trieste* actually got even deeper than *Deepsea Challenger*, at 35,814 ft (10,916 m) down, but it took five hours to make the descent and spent less than 20 minutes down there.

It took Cameron's *Deepsea Challenger* 2 hours, 37 minutes to plunge all the way down to the bottom. He reached a maximum depth of 35,787 ft (10,908 m) and spent three hours filming there, before resurfacing in less than an hour.

Voyage to the Bottom

The Challenger Deep is the deepest part of the deepest trench in the ocean—the Mariana Trench, off the Mariana Islands in the western Pacific Ocean.

Deepsea Challenger

Down she goes

Deepsea Challenger is lowered by cable from the support boat *Mermaid Sapphire*, which provides continual support and keeps in touch with the pilot through wires.

Stabilizer fin

Ocean bath foam

Deepsea Challenger's body is carved out of a material called syntactic foam. Superlight, yet stronger than steel, it not only helps the sub float back up but also provides a structure strong enough to take the incredible pressures of the deep ocean. It is made from millions of hollow glass microspheres suspended in an epoxy resin.

Hard point where a crane can grab the sub

Light in the darkness

It's pitch dark deep down in the ocean, so for Cameron to film, the sub needs lots of lights. Besides individual search lights, the sub has an 8-foot bank of superbright LEDs angled down to flood the seafloor with light.

Battery

The power for all the life-support, lighting, and camera systems comes from 70 bread loaf–sized batteries in plastic boxes on the sub's sides.

The pilot ball

The pilot is cocooned inside a tiny sphere barely 3 ft (1 m) across and has to sit with knees scrunched up for the entire voyage. It's round because a sphere is the best shape for standing up to the huge pressures of the ocean deep.

Weigh down

To pull it down to the ocean bottom, the sub has over 1,000 lb (454 kg) of solid steel plates stuck to its side by electromagnetism. To surface, the pilot simply flips a switch to turn off the electromagnets. The steel plates drop off, and the light foam body sends the sub shooting up.

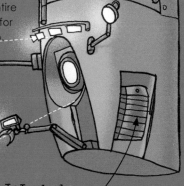

Hovercraft

If you really want to ride on air, you need a hovercraft. This craft glides on a cushion of air and is also called an air cushion vehicle, or ACV. It can travel on water and land equally easily, and it is used by the military as well as in rescue missions. The largest is the 187-ft (57-m) Russian Zubr.

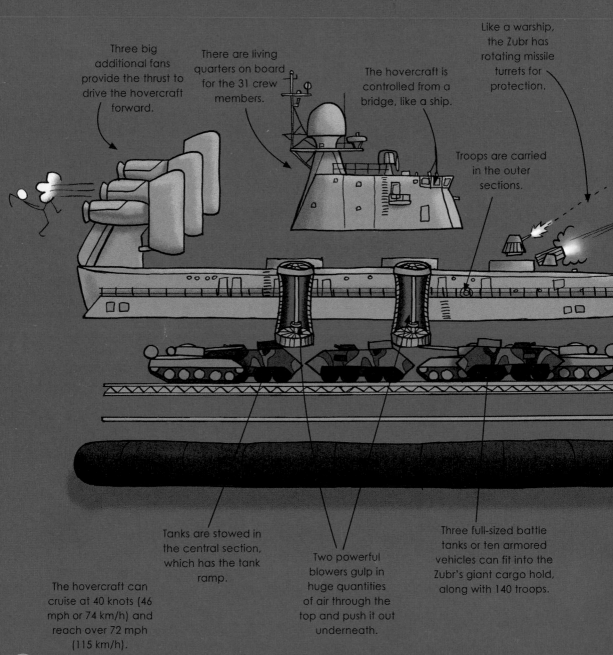

Three big additional fans provide the thrust to drive the hovercraft forward.

There are living quarters on board for the 31 crew members.

The hovercraft is controlled from a bridge, like a ship.

Like a warship, the Zubr has rotating missile turrets for protection.

Troops are carried in the outer sections.

Tanks are stowed in the central section, which has the tank ramp.

Two powerful blowers gulp in huge quantities of air through the top and push it out underneath.

Three full-sized battle tanks or ten armored vehicles can fit into the Zubr's giant cargo hold, along with 140 troops.

The hovercraft can cruise at 40 knots (46 mph or 74 km/h) and reach over 72 mph (115 km/h).

How Hovercraft Work

Hovercraft have powerful fans that draw air in through the top and out through the bottom. A fabric skirt around the edge of the bottom traps the blown air under the craft to create the cushion that lifts it up.

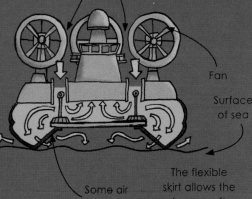

Intake – lift fan

Fan

Surface of sea

The flexible skirt allows the hovercraft to ride over obstacles.

Some air escapes

An additional fan pushes air backward to drive the hovercraft forward.

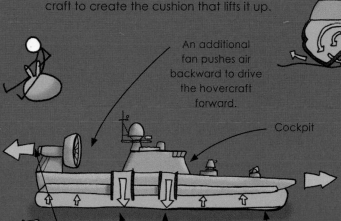

Cockpit

Air blows downward

An air cushion inside the skirt supports the craft.

A rudder behind the fan directs the air to steer the craft.

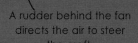

Useful Machines

The first hovercraft was invented in the 1950s by British engineer Christopher Cockerell. They are now used all around the world for everything from disaster relief to surveys, with mini versions raced as a sport.

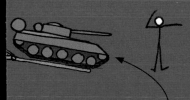

When the Zubr's ramp comes down, the tanks and troops can be out and into battle in minutes.

Zubr Craft

Because the Russian Zubr can zoom from water to land without stopping, it's perfect for a rapid invasion from the sea. It has not yet been used in battle.

Strange Inventions

People have had crazy ideas for watercraft for very many years...

Who Needs Oars or Sails?

Mechanically powered boats are nothing new. Back in the Middle Ages, numerous inventors came up with ideas for paddle-driven boats. One manuscript from that period shows a boat with multiple paddles, and animals such as cows providing the power to turn the paddles. And in one book from Roman times, there is an illustration of an ox-driven paddleboat.

Water Bike

Who said you can't ride your bike across the sea? A water bike is a boat made by attaching a bicycle to floats and connecting the pedals to paddles that drive it along. San Francisco inventor Judah Schiller created a water bike called the BayCycle and in 2013 became the first person to cross San Francisco Bay...on a bicycle.

Wavecutter

Earthrace looked more like a giant cartoon crow than a boat. It was a trimaran—a boat with three hulls. With its long, sharp nose, it was meant to slice straight through waves rather than ride over the top. The idea was to break the round-the-world speed record for a powerboat, but technical problems interrupted the record attempt. It was renamed *Ady Gil*, became involved in protests against whaling—and was then sunk by a Japanese whaling ship.

Dolphin Boat

The Innespace Seabreacher has got to be one of the most extraordinary submarines ever. It's a tiny one-person sub, shaped like a dolphin, that is powered like a Jet Ski and is completely acrobatic. As well as whizzing over the water at speeds of more than 40 mph (65 km/h), it can dive, roll, and even jump right out of the water, just like a live dolphin.

Look, Wave-Walker

The WAM-V, or Wave Adaptive Modular Vessel, looks like something from a *Star Wars* movie. It skims along on two giant inflatable tubes that independently dance up and down over the waves. That way the passengers, carried high above in a gondola supported on spiderlike legs, stay rock-steady, and only the tubes move, like giant feet.

Glossary

Bilge
The bottom of the inside of a boat's hull

Bow
The front of a boat

Bridge
The place on a large ship from which it is controlled

Catamaran
A boat with two linked hulls side by side

Chine
The bend in a hull profile

Helm
The steering of a ship

Hull
The watertight body shell of a boat

Hydrofoil
A boat that rides up out of the water on winglike foils on legs

Keel
The fin or backbone of a boat

Pilot
Expert who guides a ship

Port
The left of the ship, facing forward

Rigging
The ropes and wires that hold masts and sails up on a sailing ship

Rudder
The hinged steering blade that projects from the stern of the boat

Starboard
The right of the ship, facing forward

Stern
The back end of a boat

Tiller
A long, hinged arm for controlling the rudder

Trimaran
A boat with three linked hulls side by side

Turbine
Powerful engine that works by using pressurized gases to turn a fan blade

INDEX

The Author

John Farndon is Royal Literary Fellow at Anglia Ruskin University in Cambridge, UK. He has written numerous books for adults and children on science, technology, and nature, and been shortlisted four times for the Royal Society's Young People's Book Prize. He has recently created science stories for children for the Moscow Polytech science festival.

The Illustrator

John Paul de Quay has a BSc in biology from the University of Sussex, UK, and a graduate certificate in animation from the University of the West of England. He devotes his spare time to growing chilli peppers, perfecting his plan for a sustainable future, and caring for a small plastic dinosaur. He has three pet squid that live in the bath, which makes drawing in ink quite economical…

Picture Credits (abbreviations: t = top; b = bottom; c = center; l = left; r = right)
© www.shutterstock.com: 6 tl, 6 cr, 6 bl, 7 cl, 8 tl, 8 c, 8 cr, 8 bl, 8 br, 9 tl, 9 tr, 9 cl, 12 bl

7 tr PHOTOSVIT / Shutterstock.com, 7 br Ian Dunstar-commonswiki, 8 br chrisdorney / Shutterstock.com,
9 cl Andy Lindstone / Shutterstock.com, 9 cr rook76 / Shutterstock.com,
12 tl Leonard Zhukovsky / Shutterstock.com, 29 bl ID1974 / Shutterstock.com